Boise State University Western Writers Series   Number 61

William Saroyan

By Edward Halsey Foster

Stevens Institute of Technology

D11193558

Editors: Wayne Chatterton
James H. Maguire

Business Manager:
James Hadden

Cover Design by
Arny Skov, Copyright 1984

Illustration by Alice Notley,
Copyright 1984

Boise State University, Boise, Idaho

Printed in the United States of America by
Boise State University Printing and Graphics Services
Boise, Idaho

William Saroyan

William Saroyan

I. "Now What?"

What is there still to say about William Saroyan? Was he, after all, primarily a writer of his time—whom we read mainly to recover a sense of what his generation enjoyed? Was he, finally, as many have insisted, an entertainer, pleasant to read but easy to forget?

Saroyan's name is certainly known to those of us who care about literature in our time, but how many have recently read some (or, for that matter, *any*) of his works?

Saroyan's name is still respected; he is a writer about whom we should know something, a writer whom we *should* read. We know that *The Time of Your Life* continues to be a popular choice for repertory and amateur theatrical groups. We have heard that *The Daring Young Man on the Flying Trapeze* is among the most forceful and frightening expressions of what it meant to be alive in America in the 1930s. And we know that Saroyan refused the Pulitzer Prize because he believed business and art should not be allied. That belief must, or should, trouble any serious writer awarded a grant or prize by any foundation.

But having said these things, having summarized the conventional arguments in Saroyan's favor, we have not begun to explain why his reputation persists—why, that is, we automatically include him among the best American writers of the 1930s: James T. Farrell, John Steinbeck, Thomas Wolfe, Erskine Caldwell, John O'Hara, and others.

Among those writers, it is Saroyan who most resists definitions and categories. His writing suggests no immediate association with a particular literary or political group from the 1930s, a decade in which a writer's reputation was often defined by his political allegiances and literary friendships.

Saroyan was, first, last, and defiantly, a member of no special literary or political group, and it may, in part, be here that we can find explanations both why his writings provide great pleasure and why, in the end, they are so difficult to describe, interpret, classify, and understand in terms of the conventionally understood traditions of American literature.

A few days before his death, Saroyan called the Associated Press and dictated his "last words." Sardonically, they pointed out, one final time, that he was his own man: "Everybody has got to die, but I have always believed that an exception would be made in my case. Now what?"

Anyone who knows Saroyan's work should recognize in those words the typical Saroyan "Voice," capable, no matter what the situation, of finding something to be touched by or to laugh about. Saroyan's voice was, among his contemporaries, as distinct as Faulkner's or Hemingway's. It could be genial, warm, often sentimental, whimsical, and generous—the voice of a man who has found the world no easy place to survive but who will not give in to dejection or despair. Even in his least successful works, Saroyan generally maintained the voice of a man whom most of us would like very much to meet.

It may be that, in the end, it will be Saroyan's special voice, rather than specific works by him, that will be remembered.

Howard Floan's study of Saroyan's work carefully summarizes and generously evaluates even the least interesting books and plays, and, as Floan demonstrates, there is much in Saroyan's work that, as literature, is of little interest. Generous as Floan can be, even he does not say much good about some of the later books, such as *Not Dying*, which he dismisses as "nearly intolerable" (p. 147). Another book-by-book summary of Saroyan's career seems, at this point, unnecessary, but an examination of the major work, with attention to Saroyan's background and what he thought good literature should be, may give us a sense of why this writer at his best could be very good indeed and why his books were held in high esteem by many writers in the generation immediately following his own.

II. First Principles

Saroyan seems to have been in many ways—and it is a good thing to say it—an ordinary man; he was not a man who, by virtue of friends or family, descended from or belonged to an educated aristocracy (as did Melville, Hawthorne, Emerson, James, Faulkner, and most other major American writers), a cultural bedrock on which fiction could be built. Most American writers of stature have their origins in the middle or upper-middle classes. Saroyan was the son of refugees who settled on New York's Lower East Side in the early years of this century, and his work is pervaded by a sense of what it means to be socially and culturally invisible in America. This is, in fact, the subject of his best known story, "The Daring Young Man on the Flying Trapeze." One reason that Saroyan's early work seemed so startlingly new, even revolutionary, may be that he began with no established American tradition to rebel against or to adopt.

Among the interesting things in the works of Saul Bellow and other recent writers whose fiction is drawn from immigrant or refugee experience are the ways these works transform traditional western or American literary models to new ends: Huck Finn becomes Augie March. Saroyan's writings have their literary antecedents, but, despite Edmund Wilson's insistence that those writings gained much from Hemingway, and despite Saroyan's own insistence that his work owes much to George Bernard Shaw, his work, at its best, is unique; it has no clear-cut precedents. He could make his work conform to the traditional conventions of the short story, play, or novel; he could write like O'Henry or Zane Grey (both of whom he admired), but when he did, he did not write his best. Many of the best works—like *The Time of Your Life*—were written at white heat without much consideration for precedent.

Floan has argued that Saroyan's works "fall into four periods distinct in genre and varied in tone": 1934-1939, characterized by a truly massive production of short stories; 1939-1943, characterized by his best work for the theater; 1943-1953, characterized by prose fiction, particularly novels but including some short fiction; and a final period, "characterized by a variety of literary kinds, [but] . . . distinguished from its predecessor by the addition of autobiography" (p. 7).

These distinctions are helpful as categories for analyzing Saroyan's development as a writer, but they also suggest something about his attitude toward his work. Each of these periods begins with his best work in a particular genre—*The Daring Young Man on the Flying Trapeze* (short stories), *The Time of Your Life* (drama), *The Human Comedy* (novel), and *The Bicycle Rider in Beverly Hills* (autobiography)—and then tapers off into works that seem to have been written with too little thought; they read like literary exercises to which the author gave little effort. It is as if once Saroyan mastered a certain literary form, he lost interest in a serious way in that sort of accomplishment—or, conceivably, simply became overconfident. There are major exceptions to this pattern, but generally it holds true.

Since most of the remainder of this discussion of Saroyan's work will concentrate on the better known and more successful works, it may be helpful first to give a sense of their place in the indisputable variety and extraordinary extent of his achievement, both good and bad.

Saroyan's first success, his volume of short stories, *The Daring Young Man on the Flying Trapeze*, which we will discuss later, was followed by *Inhale and Exhale* and *Three Times Three* (both 1936). The first was a collection of stories (many of such "stories" were closer to anecdotes), some apparently autobiographical, which capitalized on successful themes from his first book, and the second was a miscellaneous collection, even less ambitious. (Indeed some of the pieces had been rejected elsewhere and might never have been published had not a new publishing enterprise given him virtual freedom to "create" a new book.) The book, however, included "The Man With His Heart in the Highlands," which would form the basis for one of Saroyan's more successful plays. Later collections include *Little Children* (1937), *Love, Here Is My Hat* (1938), *The Trouble with Tigers* (1938), and *Dear Baby* (1944). While these collections often demonstrate increased technical proficiency, they are also often shallow in characterization and facilely written. They are often about loss, disappointment, the breakdown of human possibility—dark themes and attitudes that require far greater serious consideration than they receive. One important achievement stands out among this later work, however: *My Name Is Aram* (1940), a series of interrelated stories or sketches based on Saroyan's knowledge of the Armenian community in Fresno, California. Although occasionally marred by superficial characterizations and sentimentality, the book is among Saroyan's best.

The best known of Saroyan's plays, *The Time of Your Life* (1940), will be discussed later, but mention should be made here of his other plays (most of which, stored with other manuscripts in a house Saroyan owned in Fresno, have apparently never been published or, for that matter, produced), particularly *My Heart's in the Highlands*

(1940), in which an elderly musician realizes in his music a beauty that a neglected poet has tried to realize in his own work. Essentially about the loneliness of the artist, the play, in its deeply felt pathos is among Saroyan's more effective works despite some careless or hasty writing. *Love's Old Sweet Song* (1940), in which a family of migrant workers literally take over the lives of some middle class Americans, may have been Saroyan's response to the much more sentimental portrait of migrants in Steinbeck's *The Grapes of Wrath*. Among his one-act plays (the theatrical equivalent of his short stories), *Hello, Out There* (about the murder of a falsely accused rapist) and *The Cave Dwellers* (essentially about the intensity of emotion possible for workers conventionally assumed to be "too strong" for feeling) continue to find interested readers.

The first and best known of Saroyan's novels is *The Human Comedy* (1943), to be discussed later. Other novels include *The Adventures of Wesley Jackson* (1946), a sentimental autobiographical novel based on Saroyan's army experiences. He followed this with *The Adventures of William Saroyan* (published in *The Twin Adventures*, 1950), based on his experiences writing *Wesley Jackson*. Saroyan's family life always seems to have been problematic, and in the 1950s and 1960s, he published a series of novels dealing usually with the darker side of family relations (father-son, husband-wife, etc.): *The Laughing Matter* (1953; this, the bleakest of all, dealt with adultery and the consequent breakdown of a marriage), *Mama, I Love You* (1956), *Papa, You're Crazy* (1957), *Boys and Girls Together* (1963), and *One Day in the Afternoon of the World* (1964). *Rock Wagram* (1951), concerned with an Armenian bartender who becomes famous in movies but loses his ethnic identity in the process, perhaps suggests emotional parallels to Saroyan's life. *Tracy's Tiger* (1951), the best, certainly the most whimsical, of the later novels, will be discussed below.

10

Obsessed in most of his fiction with problems of identity—personal, familial, and cultural—Saroyan turned at the end to biography and autobiography in a series of books with, unfortunately, little or no literary value. Nevertheless, his biographical writing does provide a wealth of personal detail valuable in interpreting the rest of Saroyan's career and books: *The Bicycle Rider in Beverly Hills* (1952), *Short Drive, Sweet Chariot* (1966), *I Used to Believe I Had Forever* (1968), *Letters from 74 rue Taitbout* (1969), *Days of Life and Death and Escape to the Moon* (1978), *Places Where I've Done Time* (1972), *Sons Come and Go, Mothers Hang in Forever* (1976), *Chance Meetings* (1978), and *Obituaries* (1979).

Among other works from this period is the text Saroyan did for *Look at Us* (1967), a book of photographs by Arnold Rothstein. Saroyan's text is not distinguished, but as commentary on the work of a photographer whose career, like Saroyan's, is primarily associated with the depression, it has an interest. It may not always be an interest that Saroyan intended, however. When, for example, he accompanies Rothstein's famous picture of a father and his two sons fleeing a dust storm with "Dreams are never photographed, and man's most wonderful and terrible realities are hardly ever, and then almost by accident" (p. 24), a reader may wonder if Saroyan really remembered what the horror of the depression, which he had recorded so remarkably in his first book, had been like. As in so much of Saroyan's work, the text of *Look at Us* suggests a writer who simply could not or would not give his work the attention or effort required to find the right word, the perfect phrase.

Surveying Saroyan's career as a whole, what we find is great productivity but, relative to the number of books he published, few that are of any great continuing interest. Much of the work is entertaining without making any substantial intellectual or imaginative demand on the reader, yet Saroyan can not be dismissed, together with writers like Damon Runyan and O'Henry, as merely or largely an entertainer; from time to time—as in his early stories—he wrote very well, with an acute and disturbing sense of life in his time.

If Saroyan is to be remembered among major American writers who began to publish in the 1930s, it must be for his earliest work, especially the first short stories and plays. By the time he published his first novel, he had developed an air or tone of conventional sentimental acceptance—good things are to be found everywhere, if we will only look for them—that vitiates much of the later work. Some of his writings about marriage are harsh and uncompromising, perhaps reflecting the difficulties in, and eventual failure of, his own marriage, but sentimentality and whimsy are common in the later work, and it is unpleasant for a reader who admires the early stories and plays to find himself faced with such passages as the following from *Rock Wagram* (1951):

A man's needs are few, his desires many, but one need and one desire are the same, love. But love like money is a dangerous thing and the possession of it does peculiar things to a man, as the want of it does terrible. For want of love a man may invent a religion, take to drink, or to the belittling of poets.

To be loved is to be accepted. To love is to accept. It is probably good but probably impossible to accept. (p. 29)

The year 1943 marks the end of the most successful period of Saroyan's career, which had its beginning fifteen years earlier when, not quite twenty years old, he took a bus from his home in California to New York with the perhaps heroic and adolescent vision of establishing himself as a writer in the great city.

In 1921, he had purchased his first typewriter and had begun typing out pieces for magazines. Living in the city he collected his rejection slips but was not discouraged; he would still be what he had decided to be. New York was not as eager for his literary abilities as he had expected, however, and within six months, he was back in California. But he was even more determined to succeed as a writer, and within a few years, magazines were accepting his work and soliciting more.

The public Saroyan in the 1930s was criticized by literary acquaintances for seeming too brash, aggressive, or self-centered. He was too eager, they felt, to talk about himself and his work. But in these early years, he seems also to have been so absorbed by what he wrote, so obsessed with telling the truth as he saw it, that no other behavior should have been expected. And in the end that supreme self-confidence was rewarded.

During these years Saroyan also discovered that his best subjects were himself and the people he knew well; the trouble came when he tried to widen his literary perspective and developed instead sentimental colorings and shallow insights.

To understand Saroyan, it is important to know something about his Armenian-American and his Western backgrounds, for although few of his writings, aside from the autobiographies, record specifics from his past, that past seems frequently to shape his vision of experience in his best work. To choose an obvious example, *My Name Is Aram* deals with an Armenian-American community such as the one Saroyan knew as a child, but it does not, he insists, record specific incidents of a sort he could have known; the book is a series of variations on things remembered from his childhood. Similarly, one might assume that *The Time of Your Life* is based on people or types Saroyan encountered in San Francisco, that *My Heart's in the Highlands* may in part refer to incidents in the life of Saroyan's father (who, like the play's hero, was a man with great intellectual abilities and little cash), and that *The Human Comedy* is partly a sentimental transformation of the author's memories of Fresno,

California, into an idealized American small town.

At his best, Saroyan was often, in one way or another, writing autobiography, and his final autobiographical works are logical continuations of something he had been doing from the start.

III. Armenia

To understand Saroyan, the place to begin is not America but ancient Armenia in eastern Turkey, from which his parents emigrated early in this century.

The landscape of Armenia is barren ànd dry in summer. Although once rich, fertile, and forested, the region now has few trees, and the bedouin tribes that camp here stay close to their tents, away from the burning sun.

Soviet Armenia is still occupied largely by Armenians, but few Armenians remain in the Turkish sector, the home of Saroyan's ancestors. It is a vast open land, rugged and threatening. There are a few Turkish villages with their mosques and minarets, and there are also a few Kurdish outposts and, of course, the bedouin tribes. But almost no signs exist to show that Armenians, driven out or exterminated by the massacres a few generations ago, occupied this land for nearly three thousand years.

Saroyan's ancestors came from the village of Bitlis in the Taurus mountains east of Lake Van. Now a conservative Islamic village, a hundred years ago Bitlis was an important center of Armenian culture.

Under the Ottoman Turks, Armenians became wealthy and respected merchants. (Among Turks, trade was, and to a degree still is, considered disreputable, and it was, therefore, an ideal way for Jews, Arabs, Armenians, and other minorities to succeed. It was one profession in which they would not expect persecutions.) Bitlis had been for centuries a center of trade under various Arabic, Per-

14

sian, Byzantine, and Turkish rulers, and it must have seemed a very safe and respectable place for Armenians to establish their culture.

But it was not an easy place in which to live. In *Rock Wagram*, an elderly woman remembers that "When winter came we were kept in our houses five months waiting for the snows to melt. Those five months . . . were the most terrible I have ever known, [my husband] would not be loved and said, 'Go to America, this is no place to live, this is a place to die'" (p. 74).

But for a while, Bitlis, despite its climate and isolation, at least offered a sanctuary—free, for the moment, from all the unimaginable persecutions to which Armenians had been subjected for centuries.

Then came the bloody Ottoman rule of Sultan Abdul-Hamid II with its systematic extermination of Armenians. Few escaped.

Saroyan's father, Armenak, a well-educated minister, writer, and scholar, was one of those who got out. In 1905, he and other Armenians from Bitlis arrived in New York and settled near the Bowery on the Lower East Side.

IV. Armenak

Saroyan's attitudes toward his ancestors, his family, and his father could be very ambiguous, sometimes respectful and at other times distant. In *I Used to Believe I Had Forever*, he wrote that he remembered his father "as a good man" of whom "the worst that anybody was willing to say . . . was that he was too good for this world" (p. 63). In fact, not only had his father, with little cash, been able to get himself and his family to America; he had also quickly established himself here as a writer for the *Christian Herald* and as a minister for a church in Paterson, New Jersey. In addition, he was soon well known as a poet, essayist, and public speaker. His writings were to have much importance for his son, who claimed in *The*

Bicycle Rider in Beverly Hills that one of the main reasons he became a writer was because his father had been one, too (p. 43).

On the other hand, Saroyan states in one of his last memoirs, *Sons Come and Go, Mothers Hang in Forever*, that his father was "the failed poet, the failed Presbyterian preacher, the failed American, the failed theological student" (p. 20). It is true that Armenak Saroyan, after he had established himself respectably in the East, suddenly left for California to become the minister of an Armenian church in Fresno, only to find that the congregation wanted someone who spoke Turkish, a language that he knew poorly. But the difficulties that resulted—he had to abandon his scholarly interests and, in order to support his family, take a job in the vineyards— were the accidents of fate, not personal shortcomings. Armenak Saroyan died suddenly a short time after his arrival in California, but had he lived longer, one suspects that, given his obvious ambitions and abilities, he would once again have succeeded.

Armenak's death had lasting and hated consequences for his family. His wife was unable to support their children, and they were placed in an orphanage. William Saroyan was three years old. Their mother was able to visit only on weekends. Saroyan's bitterness toward his childhood and his ambiguous attitudes toward his past may well have had more to do with the years spent in the orphanage than with his memories and impressions of his father and the Armenian community he knew in Fresno.

V. Aram vs. William

Saroyan's father named him for Dr. William Stonehill, a friend and Presbyterian minister who helped Armenian refugees in New York. Saroyan thought of himself, however, very much as an Armenian, and, had the choice been his, he would, he said, have taken the name Aram. His collection of stories based on his memories of the Armenian community in Fresno is titled *My Name Is Aram*, and Aram is the name he gave his son.

Clearly Saroyan's Armenian identification had considerable importance for him, and that fact is repeatedly emphasized by him. To choose a minor but revealing example, *Places Where I've Done Time* is dedicated to "Armenians, half Armenians, quarter Armenians, and one-eighth Armenians. Sixteenth and thirty-second Armenians, and other winners, are likelier to be happy with a useful book" (p. 5).

Perhaps the principal effect of Saroyan's Armenian heritage on his work is not be found in his use of his background for subject matter but rather in a deep, pervasive sense of being an outsider. In other words, what matters most is not so much his having been an Armenian as his having been an Armenian in America—and, therefore, instantly an eccentric, an outsider.

Armenians have for centuries been geographical and historical anomalies. Armenia was the first nation to adopt Christianity, but Armenian Christianity has always been distinct from other forms of Christianity in church structure, ritual, and belief. Because few Christian peoples live in Asia, the Armenians were surrounded by Arabs, Kurds, Turks, Persians, and other nations of Islam.

For centuries after their country was overrun by Arabs and Turks, Armenians were outsiders in their own land. In America, the situation was in some ways worse; although there were no longer threats of Turkish invasions, the immigrant Armenian was cut off from his land and his culture, for here he could find little of the Asian culture he had left behind. Immigrant cultures in America have generally been European, and so even among the immigrant cultures of the Lower East Side or Fresno, the Saroyans and other Armenians were alone.

American literature is a literature of outsiders; its finest books—

Moby-Dick, Adventures of Huckleberry Finn, and (to choose an excellent example) *Zen and the Art of Motorcycle Maintenance*—are about, and are often narrated by, outsiders. Saroyan could find within his cultural background a vision of experience that fit closely an established vision in American literature.

VI. "The Assyrian"

One of Saroyan's stories dealing explicitly with what it means to be an outsider in this world is "The Assyrian," the title piece in a collection of short fiction published in 1950. It is an exceedingly well crafted story, equal to much of F. Scott Fitzgerald's and Ring Lardner's work, and reminiscent, in its resignation to solitude as an inevitable part of experience, to Fitzgerald's "The Rich Boy."

Saroyan's story concerns an Assyrian-American (an ethnic identity even more bizarre and culturally "invisible" than Armenian-American), a famous writer who has been a loser in everything (no friends, three divorces) except gambling and his profession. Since he is a celebrity, his opinions and activities are reported in the newspapers, but no one cares much for him as a person. He simply makes good copy. The thing which gives his life an edge is gambling, and he usually wins but gains no one's admiration; all that he has to show for his life, his writing and his gambling, is money.

Saroyan said that he began the story to make money, but "the longer I worked at it, . . . the more hopeless the possibility of this financial coup became, for the writing would not be cheerful, would not be amusing, would not be something hundreds of thousands of friendly, normal, cheerful people might find in a magazine and know would be nice" (*The Assyrian,* p. xvii).

It is, however, precisely this inability to be amusing, this resistance to being merely entertaining, that raises "The Assyrian" above most of Saroyan's work and makes it such an effective short story.

At the center of the piece is the question of what marks a man—despite his public and private successes—as an outsider, a loner. Why is it that "in the end, as in the beginning, a man is alone" (p. 65)? The answer seems to lie in the man's heritage: "The longer he'd loved, the more he'd become acquainted with the Assyrian side [of himself], the old side, the tired side, the impatient and wise side, the side he had never suspected existed in himself until he was thirteen and had begun to be a man" (p. 17). Finally, obsessed with this solitude that he never chose, he asks himself why he has never been able to find close friends, and the answer comes back: "It was probably because the Assyrian side of him just naturally didn't believe in it" (p. 21). At the end of the story, he takes a plane to the Middle East and the site of a heritage and culture that, except in the solitude of his imagination and the imaginations of people from backgrounds like his, no longer exists. But he has no other way, except death, to end his solitude.

In one of his earliest stories, "Antranik of Armenia," Saroyan explicitly rejected what has always been the easiest emotional response for an oppressed race or nation: hatred for the oppressor. The Armenian, he implied, was no better and no worse than the Turk. (Cf. p. 257 of *Inhale and Exhale.*) The culture that survives because of its shared hatreds is not, he assumes, a culture worth preserving. Armenian identity had nothing to do with a common oppressor.

A man's ethnic identity, he suggested in another early short story, "The Armenian and the Armenians," had more to do with a personal awareness than with geography. Nationality or ethnicity is a matter of imagination, not territorial designations:

There is a small area of land in Asia Minor that is called

Armenia, but it is not so. It is not Armenia. It is a place . . . . There are only Armenians, and they inhabit the earth, not Armenia, since there is no Armenia . . . . There is no America and there is no England, and no France, and no Italy. There is only the earth . . . . *(Inhale and Exhale,* p. 437)

Saroyan's politics, which probably cost him much critical support and many readers in the 1930s, could conceivably have had foundations in this sense of national or ethnic identity. It is a sense which, in a pluralistic society, emphasizes individuality at the expense of any real opportunity for friendship and mutual understanding. The past, rather than the present, shapes people. It is an intensely conservative view, but one which Saroyan apparently could not avoid. In an interview with Michael J. Arlen for Arlen's study of Armenian culture today, *Passage to Ararat* (1975), Saroyan insisted that "An Armenian can never not be an Armenian" (p. 49).

While many writers in the 1930s were dedicated to the creation of a new society, Saroyan wrote about the survival of traditional values and customs both in his Armenian community and in the country at large. *The Time of Your Life* is essentially about the survival of fundamental human values: a sense of decency, fair play, civility, and generosity of spirit. Despite a national depression and the early signs of a war abroad, the people in Saroyan's play are able to ignore the world at large and create, among themselves, the kind of decent life that, the play suggests, might be possible for everyone. It is a deeply sentimental conclusion.

VII. The American West

To be a writer from the West writing about Western life could be, among the critical establishment of Saroyan's generation, no recommendation, and there is no better place to see that than

Edmund Wilson's strangely ill-tempered study of California literature, *The Boys in the Back Room* (1941). The book's very title suggests that its subject was not something to be taken altogether seriously.

What makes Wilson's book interesting for us is its provincial, Eastern attitude, derived from a formidable understanding of European and American literature on which, Wilson believed, accomplished books are built.

Wilson's less-than-generous attitude toward Western writers is evident in his comments on Robinson Jeffers: "It is probably a good deal too easy to be a nihilist [like Jeffers] on the coast at Carmel; your very negation is a negation of nothing" (p. 49). Wilson's words make effective rhetoric, but they are not true. Culture is in any case far more than geographic identity, as Saroyan insisted, and the America that Jeffers so bitterly condemned was as present in Carmel as in Wilson's New York.

We have good reason to quarrel with many of Wilson's judgments; for all the book's renown, there is something distasteful about it. Some of his assertions are simply wrong. For example, his claim that Hemingway influenced Saroyan is a statement to which Saroyan strongly objected and which still must baffle anyone interested in Saroyan's work. What could Wilson have been thinking of? Other comments only glimpse the truth.

In an attempt to describe the atmosphere that *The Time of Your Life* evokes, Wilson states that the play's "spell . . . consisted in its creating the illusion of friendliness and muzzy elation and gentle sentimentality which a certain amount of beer or rye will bring on in a favorite bar" (p. 27). And that, of course, is no justification for a great play. If it is "the illusion of friendliness and muzzy elation and gentle sentimentality" that one is looking for, then a bar would probably do as well as the play. Wilson doesn't consider the possiblity that Saroyan may have been suggesting a world in which real friendliness, not merely "the illusion of friendliness," is possible.

Wilson is close to an explanation for one aspect of Saroyan's achievement when he says that "the whole trick is in the temperament" (p. 27). Saroyan is not primarily a writer of ideas or manners. He is at his best when he records that variety of moods or temperaments from despair to exhilaration which condition the way people behave and what they believe. As another critic has put it, "Saroyan's secret is that he believes in the mood of the moment as something almost absolute, and whatever other statements he may have made, they are undoubtedly subordinate to that first principal, including even his belief in the brotherhood of Man" (Heinrich Strauman, *American Literature in the Twentieth Century*, p. 200).

Although it is this fascination with a special mood, rather than ideas or a set of customs, that makes Saroyan's work distinctive and interesting, Wilson finally concentrates too heavily on its dangers. Saroyan, he says, "seems sometimes in danger of becoming . . . the kind of columnist who depends entirely on a popular personality, the kind who never reads, who does not know anything in particular about anything, who merely turns on the tap every day and lets it run a column" (p. 29).

In his later career, Saroyan, as garrulous as many columnists, produced book after book that said little in many words, but there is little of this in his best early works. The "temperament" of the columnist is a verbal trick; it seldom reflects anything deeply and personally felt. And Saroyan's early works are intensely personal; they are an outgrowth of deeply felt circumstances.

Wilson was certainly the most incisive and influential American critic of this century, but many of his comments on Saroyan seem strangely off the mark. Saroyan deserved much better treatment than this.

VIII. The Provinces

In Saroyan's world, there is little that is permanent aside from his vaguely articulated values. It is a highly *provisional* world that he creates, a world in transition; and "temperament" or "the mood of the moment" is consequently essential as a mooring, something to grab on to. This creation of a provisional world is what we would expect from a man whose heritage involved generations of oppression and flight, but it is also a characteristic of much Western writing both by adopted Westerners such as Owen Wister and by native Westerners such as Jack London and Richard Brautigan. The East, justly or not, is conventionally associated with conservative, established, traditional customs. The West has always seemed to be the outer edge of Euro-American civilization—still dynamic, developing, and, therefore, provisional. That regional identity is essential to Saroyan's work, and it is the essence of his style.

In terms of the work itself, this Western outlook means that a writer is more interested in detailing the present, that "mood of the moment," than in meeting traditional assumptions about literature. The result is fiction intensely immediate, powerful, and convincing. Taken to the extreme, it may result in Kerouac's technique of "spontaneous prose" in which the writer records experience directly: his books are written without premeditation or revision. In focusing on Saroyan's temperament, Wilson centered on one of the principal things that makes him most distinctly Western.

IX. Fresno

The Western city that Saroyan knew best, the city in which he spent most of his life, was Fresno, California, in the San Joaquin Valley. "In Fresno," wrote Saroyan in *The Bicycle Rider in Beverly*

Hills, ". . . Armenia was not in third place among nations of the world [after England and the United States], it was in last place, if in any place at all" (p. 54). About one in five residents of the city were Armenians, most of whom worked in the orchards and vineyards. The rest of the population held the Armenians and their world in contempt. The Armenian community resisted assimilation into the rest of the community and continued to speak Armenian in their homes and to practice customs brought from Asia. The result was an enforced isolation.

"The first purpose of my life after I reached the age of ten or eleven," wrote Saroyan in *Places Where I've Done Time*, "was to get away from Fresno as soon as possible" (p. 112). After his brief stay in New York, he settled first in San Francisco and then, having made his peace with the past, returned to Fresno. Although he spent much of his life in New York and Paris, Fresno—the city in which both his Armenian and his Western characteristics had first been shaped—was his principal home and the setting for several of his better known works.

The Fresno in his books, however, is not the Fresno of his childhood; it is a city largely without prejudice—a cleaned-up version of the city from which Saroyan had escaped. If the first major criticism of Saroyan is that he wrote too much, and that he wrote it much too carelessly, the second is that he was far too capable of overlooking the unpleasant side of experience. And that is especially evident in his literary treatment of his native city.

X. Marx and the Man

Among leftist critics in the 1930s, Saroyan's Armenian background had political value. Here was another and rather exotic ingredient for the literary melting pot of recently published Irish, Jewish, Scandinavian, Italian, and Slavic writers that included

James T. Farrell, Daniel Fuchs, Louis Adamic, and Ole Rølvaag. Politics was the denominator shared by much of the acclaimed American writing of the decade. This was the era of the proletarian novel and the Group Theater, Marxist criticism and *Partisan Review*. As Mary McCarthy's *The Company She Keeps* makes clear, in some places in America to declare interest in a writer was simultaneously to advocate his politics.

Even in literary circles where an individual's politics did not seem very interesting, literature was expected to have social force, and the result was a literature largely and overtly bound to its historical moment. At no time in American history was literature so explicitly concerned with its time as it was in the 1930s.

Most American writers highly regarded in the 1930s can be grouped in one of three categories derived from distinct social perspectives: proletarian or Marxist (Josephine Herbst, Jack Conroy, Edward Dahlberg, Meyer Levin, Richard Wright, John Steinbeck, James T. Farrell, John Dos Passos), hardboiled (John O' Hara, Nelson Algren, James M. Cain, Erskine Caldwell), and satiric (J. P. Marquand, Nathaniel West, James Thurber, George Santayana). There are major exceptions, of course, writers who fit comfortably in none of these categories, and these writers include those who, by and large, continue to have the greatest interest for us today. Not only were they, on the whole, the better writers; they concerned themselves with matters of continuing interest, while their contemporaries were absorbed with issues that are of less significance today. These greater writers include William Faulkner, Wallace Stevens, Henry Miller, Hart Crane, Thomas Wolfe, and Ernest Hemingway.

Paradoxically, Saroyan, at his worst, belonged to this latter group; at his best, he was affiliated with writers concerned more directly with matters of contemporary interest—but it is essential to emphasize that he never adopted any of the commonly shared political or social theories preached by writers of his time. Saroyan's weakest books—e.g., such early collections of short stories as *Love, Here Is My Hat* and *Saroyan's Fables*—are those least tied, at least explicitly tied, to their decade. He was most successful when, as he said of *The Time of Your Life*, his work was "of our time" (p. 11).

But to write "of our time" did not, according to many of Saroyan's fellow writers, mean merely choosing a contemporary setting; it meant adopting a contemporary political stance, and that was something that Saroyan did not do. In *Three Times Three*, near the beginning of his career, he insisted that "I sincerely wish I could believe with the Communists that there is hope for the masses, but I cannot." Perhaps there was "hope for man" but only "for one man at a time" (p. 69). In his essay "William Saroyan and the Theater of Transformation" (published in Warren French's *The Thirties*) James H. Justus has suggested that as far as leftist politics of the decade were concerned, Saroyan simply did not measure up. "It was clear to The Committed," Justus wrote, "that Saroyan was not effectively angry" (p. 212).

Nonetheless, there could be no question that Saroyan wrote well— even if he did not write about the "correct" things. Perhaps a good entertainer, in the effort to re-shape American society he had no place.

Saroyan's work was also problematic when placed beside the work of more "moderate" writers, those, that is, less interested in social revolution than in a cultivation of what they considered the better aspects of the American past—particularly the traditional idealization of the "common man."

The idealization of the "common man" was conventional in the arts in the 1930s. It is found in works as otherwise diverse as Carl

Sandburg's biography of Lincoln, Aaron Copland's orchestral works "Fanfare for the Common Man" and "A Lincoln Portrait," John Steinbeck's novel *The Grapes of Wrath*, Thomas Hart Benton's murals, Frank Capra's film *Meet John Doe*, and the various state guides prepared by the Works Progress Administration—in all of which all the details of "local color," the customs of "common men," were reverently recorded. These works seem now inspired by a sentimental benignity that, by not being critical, falsifies its subject. Even the much acclaimed photographs which Dorothea Lange, Ben Shahn, Arthur Rothstein, and others took for the Farm Security Administration and which are still, on occasion, cited for their "documentary precision," turn out on close study to deal only with a narrow band of experience in the 1930s. They settle for images that show a heroic persistence or endurance in the face of hard times. They seldom show the despair, the collapse of will, among those who had given up.

Saroyan in the early part of his career was much involved with this sentimental treatment of the common man, but he could be critical of it, too. *Love's Old Sweet Song* was attacked for its harsh characterization of migrant workers, whom Saroyan portrayed as people who, whatever they have suffered, are no more moral or ideal than anyone else. In the play, they are followed around by a photographer and a journalist who try to transform them into good copy. Saroyan was making a valid point about ways in which fact is transformed for political and journalistic ends, but it was not a point that many of his contemporaries wanted to hear. Saroyan might have argued that at home in the San Joaquin Valley, with an economy dependent on migrant labor, he had much opportunity to know what the migrants were really like, but one imagines that had he argued this, it wouldn't have done much good. Whether or not his characterizations were accurate, he was writing against the political sensibility of his age.

Despite his specific criticism of the migrant workers, Saroyan was one of the principal purveyors of the 1930s' idealization of the common man. Long after others had turned to other interests, Saroyan continued in fact to idealize him in stories, novels, and plays. Certainly *The Time of Your Life* depends in part on this concern for ordinary men and women. In *The Human Comedy* Saroyan made the "common man" his principal subject, and it is a highly optimistic picture, worthy of Carl Sandburg. Indeed, the high ideals preached in that novel must have astonished readers and critics accustomed to the bleaker worlds that Saroyan had devised in *Love's Old Sweet Song* and *The Daring Young Man on the Flying Trapeze*.

XI. The Private Voice

"Art," wrote Saroyan in his introduction to *Three Plays*, "can no longer be contemptuous of politics . . ." (p. 3). (Surely a statement to raise critical eyebrows, since at no time had art been less contemptuous of politics than the 1930s; either Saroyan was saying something too obvious to be said, or he was about to insist on a very different interpretation of conventional literary dogma.) He later noted that "the imperative requirement of our time is to restore faith to the mass and integrity to the individual" (p. 60).

Saroyan sounds like a proletarian novelist, but he was using the language to suggest a very different view of society than critics and readers might have expected. Saroyan's redemption of society was to be accomplished not by political or mass action but through the redemption of the individual. Saroyan clearly did not see the individual as primarily part of a social complex, as someone who would regain his integrity through a just social order. The problem did not begin on the outside, in the world of shared experience and

28

values, but within the private, secret world of the self.

And Saroyan's literary voice is the example. While some of his contemporaries borrowed an impersonal literary voice from journalism, Saroyan cultivated a highly personal vocabulary and attitude. This special voice was in turn the medium through which the historical moment could be interpreted. Instead of insisting on an objective reality to be interpreted through a political ideology or system, he recorded the world according to a personal, idiosyncratic perspective expressed through his literary voice: sentimental, generous, genial, warm, whimsical, amused, and amusing.

Saroyan's literary voice and the political position that it implies seem logical extensions of his regional and ethnic heritage. If he had wanted, he could have found in contemporary politics revenge or solution for the class, ethnic, and regional difficulties he encountered. As a Western writer trying to establish a reputation in a profession dominated by Eastern publishers and critics, as a relatively uneducated writer—his formal education ended with high school—in a profession increasingly controlled by university-trained men and women, and, above all, as an Armenian, he would certainly have been justified in aligning himself with polemical writers on the left. But that would have meant transforming himself into an entirely different sort of man and, ironically, abandoning his personal, individual values. What he did was locate a literary voice that, in its sincerity and warmth, is among the most distinctive and pleasant of his generation's. Although a critical reader may find little of literary value in Saroyan's later works, he will still have the pleasure of listening to a very good and charming man talk.

XII. What Art Does

If, by his own admission, Saroyan wrote much for money, he also wrote conscientiously and honestly. Writing, as his various autobiographies make clear, was of high seriousness for him.

To understand his accomplishment, it is helpful to understand what he personally expected from his work and what the profession of writing meant to his generation. To begin, we might reflect on the enormous productivity of writers who matured professionally during the depression. Faulkner is the most obvious example of one who, simply in terms of the number of works that he published, was prolific in a fashion seldom encountered among earlier American writers. This was also the decade of gargantuan, endlessly garrulous popular novels like Hervey Allen's *Anthony Adverse* and Margaret Mitchell's *Gone with the Wind*. Many proletarian novels were vast and literally weighty affairs. Anyone planning to read his way through the complete works of James T. Farrell or Thomas Wolfe is faced with a formidable project. Legend has it that Wolfe sent the manuscript of one of his novels to his editor in a truck, and the editor chopped the manuscript severely, returning the abbreviated version in the back seat of a taxi.

The minutely crafted work of, say, Hawthorne was being replaced by an aesthetic that would culminate a generation later in Jack Kerouac's "spontaneous prose" and Allen Ginsberg's famous dictum "First thought best thought." In the work of a great writer like Kerouac (or Saroyan), the result was fiction of a high order, but, of course, for a less talented imagination, this new aesthetic would mean pages and pages of unreadable prose.

While some writers in the 1930s wrote voluminously, inspired more perhaps by a desire to "get it all down" than by a desire to get it down well, a critical school—the New Criticism—was shaped around the assumption that the great literary work manifests certain formal, objectively ascertainable properties, that it can be evaluated in terms of conventions of form and technique. In this fashion, the study of literature became the study of its formal properties, and so a more conventional or traditional writer was necessarily more interesting than one who, like Saroyan or Farrell or Wolfe, might have agreed with Robert Creeley and Charles Olson that "Form is never more than an extension of content." Saroyan and his contemporaries were working in opposition to a new critical temperament, and that, as much as anything, may explain why it has taken them so long to get a fair critical hearing. It should be clear that a writer like Saroyan is not to be judged by conventional standards; the only appropriate standards are, in the end, the standards his work itself proposes.

XIII. The Writer Alone

In an essay entitled "What Makes American Writing American," Saroyan refused to place Emerson first, where he is generally placed, in the development of a specifically American literature. Saroyan argued that American writing did not begin until "the unschooled took to the business" (*I Used to Believe I Had Forever*, p. 134). Hawthorne could not be placed first, nor even Thoreau, despite his claim that his Harvard education was no education at all. Saroyan's choice was Whitman, although he "belonged to no school, and founded none" (p. 138). The American tradition did not have to do with "schools" or conventions, Saroyan argued, but rather with isolated individuals, "loners." This idea led him to list his selection of great American writers, a list especially curious in that those who are included seem to have nothing in common except that many of them were "unschooled" and most could, in one way or another, be considered "loners": among others, Ambrose Bierce, Ezra Pound, Jack London, and Theodore Dreiser.

Saroyan's essay may suggest something of his own values—that American literature should not be the product of convention or tradition and that it should be the product of solitude, the expression, that is, of an individual rather than a group. Perhaps this view may be carried one step further to the assumption that the writer should remain faithful to his private vision of the way things are, rather than to a shared standard or perspective. As a result, what matters in the work is less what the writer writes about than his attitude toward it. In a sense, this belief is merely one aspect of that concern for "the mood of the moment" that characterizes so much of what Saroyan wrote.

Writing seems to have had deeply personal, perhaps even therapeutic, values for Saroyan—as various comments throughout his career imply. In *The Bicycle Rider in Beverly Hills*, he wrote that he "was bitterly unhappy as a small child" (p. 37) and that "what I wanted was to be entire and whole" (p. 29). With that in mind, it is not surprising to find him claiming that "the object of one's activity in life, . . . is to achieve personal wholeness, and to give the material world reality and order" (*Three Times Three*, p. 137) and that "any sensible man has no choice but to invent himself, or at any rate to add invention to what is already there . . ." (*Sons Come and Go*, p. 16). In that process, literature could presumably have a substantial role, and indeed, "Art," he wrote, "begins by being a personal exercise in grace for its creator" (*Three Plays*, pp. 7-8). "Only art," he wrote in his first book, "is everlastingly dependable" (*Daring Young Man*, p. 86).

The success of a work had much to do with whether or not it possessed "wholeness" (*Three Times Three*, p. 159)—whether or not, that is, it fulfilled its own conditions. It was the sense of completeness, of form, that mattered; "form," he argued, "is our only truth, or noblest objective in art and life . . ." (*Three Times Three*, p. 99). In saying this, however, Saroyan was not aligning himself with the survivors of *l'art pour l'art*. Whatever his personal, private reasons for writing, for obtaining, through art, this "whole-

32

ness," the ultimate function of art was communal or political—though not, of course, political in the way that most leftist writers of the 1930s intended: "Art always has a better chance of having whole and unbroken form than the living have," he said, "but the only reason to achieve this unbroken form is to encourage its achievement in the living" (*Razzle Dazzle*, p. 318).

Although art may have this political function, providing, that is, a model for experience, Saroyan would not permit or condone the writer's adopting a messianic role; his job was not to teach. (See, for example, his comments on this in *The Assyrian*, p. xxxiv.) The writer was not to be didactic; he was not to tell others how to live; and here Saroyan was merely being true to his own practice, his refusal to join with leftist writers and give his work a polemical, Marxist force. Literature presented, rather, a mirage of completeness and form, a sense of wholeness that life itself did not provide, but which, nonetheless, was worth trying to find. Literary art gave life its object or point.

Saroyan's works occasionally attack repressive didactic, social, and political positions, but these attacks seem to result not from a special ideology but from a clear dislike of, or disagreement with, those positions that narrow or restrict human experience and opportunity. In the America of the 1930s, "money" and "work" were the code words around which politics turned; the problems which had to be solved were economic. But "Money," as one of the characters in *My Heart's in the Highlands* insists, "isn't everything" (p. 44). A businessman in the play claims that "You got to go out and make your living in this country. Everybody's got to work in America" (p. 39). But there is nothing in the play to suggest that the businessman is right. The play's main character is a poet who has to send his son to the local grocery store to beg for credit; there is no cash left even for essentials. At first, the father may seem irresponsible, but during the play, it becomes obvious that he has far more of value to offer as a poet than he would if he were out earning what others in the play consider a decent income. Today, two generations later, *My Heart's in the Highlands* makes an obvious point, but when it was first produced in 1939, a time when literature was conventionally fashioned for ideological ends—this was the year of Steinbeck's *The Grapes of Wrath* and (a most political work) Mitchell's *Gone with the Wind*—Saroyan was saying something as disturbing to the political left as to the political right.

Saroyan's politics, his theories of art, and his regional and ethnic identities are parts of a complex literary presence, which transforms what are, at times, rather conventional plots and characters into an accomplished literature. This is, of course, especially true when the subject is the outsider or loner, a traditional subject in American literature but one for which Saroyan's background gave him a special understanding. Saroyan's works, especially those done late in his career, are often disappointing, and it is true that he wrote no masterpiece. Yet as long as the distinctive Saroyan voice is speaking, he is worth hearing; the literary presence or personality compensates even for hasty and shallow writing. He is interesting even when what he writes is not.

To understand the range of Saroyan's work at his best and to understand ways in which Saroyan's literary presence shapes his work, it is helpful to turn to his best known works in the various genres that he cultivated: the short story ("The Daring Young Man on the Flying Trapeze"), the drama (*The Time of Your Life*), and the novel (*The Human Comedy*).

XIV. The Daring Young Man

"The Daring Young Man on the Flying Trapeze," the title piece and best story in Saroyan's best collection, can help us understand, better than any of his other early pieces, what it was that he could do so well and what it was, in turn, that led critics to include him among the most promising writers of his time. The story concerns a twenty-two-year-old writer who has no hope of finding work and no financial resources except for a penny that he finds during a walk around his city. The world about him seems cold, callous, and insensitive, and standing on a hill overlooking his city (which, like the writer, is unnamed), he feels "suddenly outside of it all." He has "somehow . . . ventured upon the wrong earth, or perhaps into the wrong age, and now . . . [is] to be permanently ejected from it" (pp. 20-21). He tries again to find work, fails, and returns to his room where, totally without help or resources, he dies of starvation.

In general, little about the story is strikingly unusual; the opposition of the aspiring writer to his indifferent society was a literary convention long before Saroyan used it. It was in fact a commonplace in the literature of the aesthetes, the decadents, and the *fin de siecle* in general. Many writers, above all James Joyce, had dealt with the real and imagined sufferings of young men and had done so at far greater length and with far greater insight than Saroyan was able to do in the brief nine pages of his sketch. The stream-of-consciousness passage with which the story begins is poor Faulkner or Joyce; it is no more than a collage of references ("laughter and mirth, satire, the end of all, of Rome and yes of Babylon," etc., p. 17), which has no special order and which tells us little about the man who thinks them except that his imagination is constructed from literature—that he is, in short, the sort of man that the rest of the story indicates.

At first glance, there would seem little reason to remember the story, and yet it is one of Saroyan's few works that is inevitably remembered and commented on in general surveys of his career. In his study of Saroyan, Howard Floan gives the story about as much attention as he gives some of the major novels and plays, and general surveys of Saroyan's work generally point to the story as an example of his best. Clearly the story has a value for its readers that transcends its many shortcomings.

The story's strength, its power over our imaginations, seems to lie in the fact that it presents itself in a hard, direct, almost journalistic fashion. It is narrated largely in the typical Saroyan voice, yet there is none of Saroyan's sentimentality or whimsy here. In *My Heart's in the Highlands*, Saroyan also dealt with the indifference of the world toward the artist; the play is in part polemic, indicting the world for its indifference. There is none of that in the story, however—no expressed indignation, no sense of injustice, no polemic. "The Daring Young Man on the Flying Trapeze" is less concerned with the world's indifference than with the writer's reaction to it. The writer asks for no sympathy or pity. He is aware that he is simply the victim of circumstances over which he has no control, and confronted with that fact, the best he can do is practice a stoic resignation. Neither polemics nor self-pity would serve a useful end.

But if "The Daring Young Man on the Flying Trapeze" concerns a writer's reaction to the indifference of the world, it is also about the indifference of American society to those who suffered most during the depression. The commonly heard statement that "no one has starved yet" was both untrue and beside the point. There was considerable suffering in America, and as yet, little was being done to help not only the writers but also the typists, secretaries, administrators, teachers, and salesmen who simply could not find work.

The writer in the story is "very angry that there [is] no respect for men who [write]" (p. 24), but he does not have any political solution to his problem. For him, as for the hundreds of thousands of other Americans who could not find work, only resignation made sense.

36

Anger was inevitably impotent anger—there was nothing the individual could do to alter the nation's economics. If there is anything heroic in the writer, it is his perfect stoic resignation in the face of circumstance over which he has no control. He has withdrawn from society. He has no friends, no resources. But in his solitude, he is free, obligated to no one.

Saroyan's story is a cold look at individual freedom and what it implies in hard times. It is one thing to insist on freedom when opportunities and cash are abundant, but it is something quite different to insist on freedom when cash is scarce. The writer makes his choice and pays an enormous price for it, but there is no indication that we should not think that his choice was the right one.

Saroyan's most interesting works are usually those about men who prefer their freedom at any cost rather than compromise with their societies. What makes his stories about outsiders and loners especially compelling is his refusal, at least in his early works, to make them seem more than they are—to give them, that is, heroic qualities that they would not be likely to possess. In his own way, Saroyan can be as unflinching and direct as such hard-boiled writers as James M. Cain and Raymond Chandler. No one reading "The Daring Young Man on the Flying Trapeze" would have been liable to guess that its author within a few years would be writing such sentimental works as *The Adventures of Wesley Jackson* and *Tracy's Tiger*.

XV. The Time of Your Life

Other stories in *The Daring Young Man on the Flying Trapeze* and in the collections which Saroyan published in the next half-dozen years (*Inhale and Exhale, Three Times Three, Love, Here Is My Hat*, among others) are frequently clever and entertaining, but many, however amusing, are merely competent, an excuse for easy reading. Saroyan, who could write too much and too hurriedly, turned out five hundred short stories (by his own count) between 1934 and 1939. *My Name Is Aram*, his collection of short stories based on his memories of his boyhood in the Armenian community in Fresno, has more interest than many of his works at this time, but it is marred by persistent nostalgia, sentimentality, and superficial characterizations. More memorable than many of the other collections largely because of its subject matter, the stories are better crafted than some of his other work at the time, but they are simply too easy to read. They don't say enough to evoke a permanent interest.

Problems in treatment and tone, particularly the excessive sentimentality, that are common in later Saroyan works are already evident in *The Time of Your Life*, his best known work and one of the major achievements of American drama in the depression era. Some important American plays of this time were excessively political, generally Marxist, in theme. For a playwright like Clifford Odets, theater became an ideological experience, but that sort of experience Saroyan did not provide. *The Time of Your Life* is set, however, in the sort of place that we might expect from a play by someone like Odets—a dockside bar, Nick's Saloon, where the rich are interlopers and the poor are able to pursue their sense of a better life. The characters—figures one might expect to find in a "realistic" Hollywood film of the time like *Sullivan's Travels*—include Willie, a pin-ball addict; Kitty Duval, a street-walker; Wesley, a black boy with musical talent but no future; and McCarthy, a longshoreman who, muscular and young in his black denim jeans and blue workshirt, suggests all the heroic qualities, and the intelligence, that the political left conventionally attributed to workers.

But Saroyan did not, of course, embrace the politics of the left in the theater, and his play may be seen, in part, as a response to dramatists like Odets. In Saroyan's play, for example, McCarthy is not cast in the role of a leader of workers—nor is it a role that he would want. He accepts what he is and asks for nothing more: ". . . all the McCarthys," he says, "are too great and too strong to be heroes. Only the weak and unsure perform the heroic. They've got to. The more heroes you have, the worse the history of the world becomes" (p. 91).

Gradually, one becomes aware that the dockside bar is not a place into which loners and the dispossessed have been forced but rather a refuge that they have chosen willingly. The best life is not heroic or ambitious or, at least in a monetary or material way, necessarily rewarding. The best life may be a sentimental retreat in which people's beliefs and ideals are seldom on the line. A character like the play's Kit Carson is able to tell stories about his perhaps imagined past to sympathetic audiences; streetwalkers like Kitty Duval can pretend for a moment that they are really ladies; and would-be comedians like Harry can momentarily find an audience for their not-very-funny routines. Instead of being an indictment of society, "Nick's Pacific Street Saloon, Restaurant, and Entertainment Palace" is an example of the way things should be. The dispossessed victims of the depression were apparently not so unfortunate after all. The play, in short, offers a sentimental view of experience—a pleasant picture that does not solve, nor honestly respond to, the problems of America at the time. In the end, Harry still won't be able to get a job, and all that Kit Carson will be able to do is, once again, tell his stories to someone with nothing to do but listen.

No matter what reservations one has about the play, however, *The Time of Your Life* does make very effective theater. It moves swiftly and, if one is not too critical, convincingly. Like such films as John Ford's *The Grapes of Wrath*, its "realism" is not very realistic, but it moves so quickly, offering so many distinctive characters, that an audience is, for the time, enchanted.

XVI. The Human Comedy

A few years after *The Time of Your Life* was produced, Saroyan offered the public another world that seemed to survive on its own merits with little or no help from people with money and power. The great problem with which the average American now had to deal was not economic depression but war, and *The Human Comedy* in effect proposed the same solution that the play had—a withdrawal from politics and the creation of a private world in which personal values and ambitions are admired. For people without power, the book and the film based on it must have been reassuring; both were enormously popular.

The Human Comedy, Saroyan's first novel, began as a screenplay for MGM, and the film, which starred Mickey Rooney, was among the studio's most profitable ventures in 1943, the year it was released. Saroyan had asked to direct it, but the studio refused, and he got revenge of a sort by turning the screenplay into a novel that was well received and, among readers of fiction, probably as popular as the film. (This was long before the era of "novelizations.")

The book continues to be popular, especially in high schools, and is available in a cheap paperback edition. In its slight, unpretentious fashion, it documents an America of small towns and friendly neighbors. There is little here to offend anyone.

The Human Comedy concerns an adolescent boy, Homer Macauley, who helps support his widowed mother and her other children during the war by working as a messenger boy for the local telegraph office. The Macauleys live in Ithaca, a small city which Saroyan seems to have loosely patterned on Fresno. The book follows Homer, his friends, and his family through various conflicts and difficulties in which they all prove themselves decent, virtuous, generous, and kind.

Although based on Fresno, Saroyan's Ithaca is recognizably the kind of fictional town that filmmakers and minor novelists like Sterling North were exploiting in the 1930s and 1940s. It is, in short, the America of Andy Hardy and his gang, where all problems are resolved amicably and justly—an America in which there are happy solutions for nearly everything. At the end of *The Human Comedy*, for example, on the same day that Homer's brother is reported killed in action, a friend from the Army arrives in Ithaca to live with the Macauleys and be a sort of replacement brother and son. Events are manipulated, as in such books of the period as North's *So Dear to My Heart* (1947) and Marjorie Kinnan Rawling's *The Yearling* (1938), to make life seem better or more orderly than it is.

Saroyan said in the dedication to the novel that he wanted it to be "the very best that I might ever be able to write," and he apparently held the book in high esteem. Much of his later work is similar to it—sometimes whimsical (as in *Tracy's Tiger*), sometimes veering off to that "impulse toward self-befuddling and self-protective fantasy" that Edmund Wilson found in parts of *The Adventures of Wesley Jackson* (*Classics and Commericals*, p. 328), and usually reaffirming an optimistic faith in human capabilities. That humanity, by and large, inevitably creates its own difficulties and sufferings is not something that Saroyan considers very often.

The Human Comedy seems based on the assumption that the great problems of humanity have already been resolved in small-town America. The small town is seen in fact as the repository of much that is best in western civilization. Ithaca is a utopia partly because it has sifted out from the past that which is good. The rest of the world, fighting a largely meaningless war, invades Ithaca's peace, but the town has ways of healing its wounds quickly.

For example, at one point an extraordinarily belligerent young man ("I can't live the kind of life I want to live and I don't feel like living any other kind," etc., p. 105) tries to hold up a clerk in the telegraph office. But the clerk insists that the boy take the money "not because you're holding a gun at me . . . [but] because you need it" (p. 4). We are then asked to believe that the boy doesn't really want the money and never did; he only wanted to discover if the clerk were really as decent as he was generally said to be. Compounding absurdity with absurdity, Saroyan has the boy and the clerk go on to talk about literature and particularly the boy's sometime delight in William Blake's "stuff" (p. 106).

The classical Ithaca is traditionally the home of Odysseus, and Saroyan's Ithaca is made up of wanderers, immigrants whose odysseys have brought them from all over the world to this place where, in the midst of a war that none of them really seem to understand or deeply support, they can preserve the remnants of their cultures. Saroyan may have been aware that Odysseus, despite his reputation as a warrior, did everything he could, including pretending to be insane, to avoid fighting at Troy.

There are many classical references in the novel. The messenger boy is fittingly named Homer. His brother, always in search of new experiences, is given Odysseus' Roman name, Ulysses. When August ("Auggie") Gottlieb leads his gang of neighborhood boys on an expedition to an orchard where he steals one of the apricots, the reference is to an incident recounted by St. Augustine (hence "August Gottlieb") in his *Confessions*. But it says much about the moral and social vision of *The Human Comedy* that while St. Augustine uses his episode to suggest that even the smallest theft is a moral problem for the Christian, Saroyan's novel suggests that

"Auggie" has not really done anything serious. It was just boys having fun, and in fact, the owner of the orchard, "old man Henderson," was more amused than angered by the boys. As usual in *The Human Comedy*, everything works out well in the end.

Apparently the only evil in Ithaca is prejudice or bigotry, and even that is not a terribly serious matter. The local bigot is the high school coach, who calls one of the students a "wop" and is properly chastised for it. A history teacher, in case anyone has missed the point, tells her students that "to be civilized" is to "respect one another" (p. 57). It is a mild way to put the matter, considering Saroyan's Armenian background and considering what was happening in Germany at this time.

The book also contains its own peculiar and unpleasant prejudices—or so it would seem today. Perhaps readers in 1943 were less startled than readers would be today by a pair of contrasting chapters dealing with women. In the first, an ambitious, accomplished, learned woman is dismissed as "horse-faced, dried out, tall, gaunt, and sexless" (p. 144). In the next chapter, we meet the madam of the "Bethel Rooms," who wants only "to make our boys happy" (p. 148). Astonishing, astonishing. One hopes that we will not encounter that sort of contrast in fiction again.

The literary sins of William Saroyan—sentimentality, whimsy, superficial characterizations, improbable plots—permeate *The Human Comedy*. Had he never written another story or novel, these shortcomings might reasonably be attributed to the fact that the book had begun as a screenplay and its literary sins were conventional in Hollywood films in the 1930s and 1940s, but within a few years, Saroyan had produced another novel, *The Adventures of Wesley Jackson*, that had at least as many problems. Although one may have reservations about Edmund Wilson's comments on Saroyan in *The Boys in the Back Room*, one can only agree with his conclusions in his review of the novel. "There is a chapter," says Wilson at the end of his review, "in which Wesley recapitulates practically every thing that has happened in the book and cries over them, including every individual who has at any time affected him unpleasantly. This is surely some of the silliest nonsense ever published by a talented writer" (*Classics and Commercials*, p. 330).

An example of Saroyan's popular later fiction is a slight, short novel he published in 1951, *Tracy's Tiger*. He thought well enough of it to include it in *The Saroyan Reader*, a selection from his works that was published in 1958. Charming and pleasant to read, the story concerns Tracy, a young man who may (or may not) have a pet tiger; we never know for sure. A psychiatrist concludes that Tracy "is obviously deluded" (p. 82), but Saroyan is on Tracy's side and concludes, for the sake of those who doubt that the tiger is real, that this affectionate man's pet is really "love" (p. 148). Readers who feel that they have been cheated by a sentimental sleight-of-hand may find at least some explanation for the book's shortcomings in the fact that, despite its popularity, it was completed, together with two other books, in thirty-one days.

XVII. Alone Again

Among the last books that Saroyan wrote, those which are likely to continue to interest readers are his many strictly autobiographical works. None possess great literary merit, but most are pleasant, and none are difficult, to read. At their worst, they are garrulous but inoffensive; at their best, they are amusing and give us much information about Saroyan's background that helps in understanding the person behind his distinctive literary voice.

During the later years, Saroyan was increasingly disregarded by critics, and so his apparent influence on writers from the next generation went largely unnoticed. In 1975, however, Michael J.

Arlen in *Passage to Ararat*, originally published in *The New Yorker*, made an important observation about that influence. Referring to a story in *My Name is Aram*, "Five Ripe Pears," Arlen wrote that "It was not an important story, but it was a lovely story—a story with a voice. It made one think with a kind of pleasure that J.D. Salinger must have heard that voice, and Richard Brautigan, and Jack Kerouac, and all those writers of the personal sound, the flower writers, the writers of our modern Era of Feeling" (p. 48).

The evidence suggests that Arlen's observation is one that we must seriously consider.

In 1967, the poet Ted Berrigan interviewed Jack Kerouac for the "Writers at Work" series in *The Paris Review*. Berrigan brought with him Saroyan's son Aram, an important poet in his own right. During the interview, Kerouac said, as indeed he had said many times before, that his literary style, particularly his aesthetic of spontaneous prose, had been inspired by the work of his friend Neal Cassady, but there were others, including Ernest Hemingway, Thomas Wolfe, and William Saroyan, who had indelibly influenced his work. With Saroyan's son there, it was a good occasion to talk especially about Saroyan's influence, and Kerouac noted, ". . . yes I loved him as a teenager, he really got me out of the 19th century rut I was trying to study, not only his funny tone but his great Armenian poetic I don't know what . . . he just got me . . ." (Kerouac, *On the Road*, Viking critical edition, p. 555).

A connection between Saroyan and the Beat writers has been suggested before. See, for example, Elaine Mary Stern's dissertation, "The Conservative Response Amidst Decades of Change: Jack Kerouac and William Saroyan." But that connection needs to be underscored as one of the truly significant lines of influence in American literary history of our time. The Beats and Saroyan shared a resistance to formal, traditional literary standards. It is worth repeating Kerouac's claim that it was Saroyan who "really got me out of the 19th century rut I was trying to study . . . ." In particular, they rejected the literary standards codified by academics and the New Criticism. There is also a shared neo-Romantic sense that literature is, from the first, personal expression and that what a writer should achieve is a unique, personal "voice" rather than a style based on respected literary antecedents. In both Saroyan (at least the early Saroyan) and the Beats, there is profound respect for populist American values accompanied by the feeling that these have been betrayed, often by those with money and power. And there is, too, the special understanding of the loner, the outsider, an empathy that is perhaps partly the result of being an immigrant or the child of immigrants—of being Armenian like Saroyan, Italian like Gregory Corso, Jewish like Allen Ginsberg, French-Canadian like Kerouac. On the one hand, immigrant status may cut the writer off from some aspects of a shared American past, but in giving him instead a fuller knowledge of that type of person most characteristic of Americans, the loner, it may provide the more valuable insights.

It is, above all, significant that the early Saroyan, like the Beats, found America valuable not in its institutions but in the unprecedented liberty which it offered the individual. While Saroyan's contemporary writers were trying to find solutions for the nation's problems through social means, he and a very few others, of whom Thomas Wolfe is an obvious example, dealt with the individual's survival and tended to consider institutions and ideologies suspect. That is, of course, a difficult and lonely position to occupy, and if Saroyan eventually idealized the small American town, as he did in *My Name Is Aram* and *The Human Comedy*, one should not be too surprised or be too harsh in criticizing him. His solitary position could not have been an easy place to accept and defend.

Many of the traits that characterize Saroyan's early heroes, including their fierce self-determination, might be dismissed as adolescent—but perhaps only in a society that values the institution and conformity over the individual and freedom. When the Beats looked back at the generation immediately preceding theirs, Saroyan was one of few welcome breaks in that grey literary landscape portraying and preaching social obligation and reform. Saroyan provided one of the few examples of a writer who was willing at that moment to insist that America's survival had more to do with its people, understood as individuals, than with its politics.

Saroyan's early accomplishment is substantial both within itself and in its apparent effect on subsequent writers. Although he later became very much an entertainer, writing books which charmed many and, since they raised few difficult questions, offended few, he created in his earlier efforts, going against the politics of his time, a substantial literature of freedom. For that and for his distinctive voice, Saroyan must be given major focus when the definitive literary history of America in the 1930s and 1940s is written.

Selected Bibliography

The following lists only the first editions of major works. Reprints, foreign editions, and ephemera have been excluded. Readers looking for a good cross section of Saroyan's work should turn to *The William Saroyan Reader* (New York: George Braziller, 1958).

PRIMARY SOURCES

The Adventures of Wesley Jackson. New York: Harcourt, Brace, 1946.
The Assyrian and Other Stories. New York: Harcourt, Brace, 1950.
The Bicycle Rider in Beverly Hills. New York: Charles Scribner's Sons, 1952.
Boys and Girls Together. New York: Harcourt, Brace, 1963.
The Cave Dwellers. New York: G.P. Putnam's Sons, 1958.
Chance Meetings. New York: Norton, 1978.
The Daring Young Man on the Flying Trapeze and Other Stories. New York: Random House, 1934.
Days of Life and Death and Escape to the Moon. New York: Dial Press, 1970.
Dear Baby. New York: Harcourt, Brace, 1944.
The Dogs; or, The Paris Comedy and Two Other Plays. New York: Phaedra, 1969.
Don't Go Away Mad and Two Other Plays. New York: Harcourt, Brace, 1949.
Get Away Old Man. New York: Harcourt Brace, 1944.
Harlem as Seen by Hirschfeld. New York: The Hyperion Press, 1941.
Here Comes, There Goes, You Know Who. New York: Simon and Schuster, 1961.
Hilltop Russians in San Francisco. San Francisco: James Dellein, 1941.
The Human Comedy. New York: Harcourt, Brace, 1943.
I Used to Believe I Had Forever; Now I'm Not So Sure. New York: Cowles, 1968.
Inhale and Exhale. New York: Random House, 1936.
Jim Dandy: Fat Man in a Famine. New York: Harcourt, Brace, 1947.
The Laughing Matter. Garden City, N.Y.: Doubleday, 1953.
Letters from 74 rue Taitbout. New York: World Publishers, 1969.
Little Children. New York: Harcourt, Brace, 1937.
Look at Us. New York: Cowles, 1967.
Love, Here Is My Hat. New York: Modern Age Books, 1938.
Mama, I Love You. Boston: Little, Brown, 1956.
Morris Hirshfield. New York: Frano Maria Ricci, 1976.

My Name Is Aram. New York: Harcourt, Brace, 1940.
A Native American. San Francisco: George Fields, 1938.
Not Dying. New York: Harcourt, Brace, 1963.
Obituaries. Berkeley, CA.: Creative Arts Book Co., 1979.
Once Around the Block. New York: Samuel French, 1959.
One Day in the Afternoon of the World. New York: Harcourt, Brace, 1964.
Papa, You're Crazy. Boston: Little, Brown, 1957.
Peace, It's Wonderful. New York: Modern Age Books, 1939.
The People with Light Coming out of Them. New York: The Free Co., 1941.
Places Where I've Done Time. New York: Praeger, 1972.
Razzle Dazzle. New York: Harcourt, Brace, 1942.
Rock Wagram. Garden City, N.Y.: Doubleday, 1951.
Saroyan's Fables. New York: Harcourt, Brace, 1941.
Short Drive, Sweet Chariot. New York: Phaedra, 1966.
The Slaughter of the Innocents. New York: Samuel French, 1958.
Sons Come and Go, Mothers Hang in Forever. New York: McGraw-Hill, 1976.
A Special Announcement. New York: House of Books, 1940.
*Three Plays: The Beautiful People, Sweeney in the Trees, Across the Board on Tomorrow
    Morning*. New York: The Free Company, 1941.
Three Plays: My Heart's in the Highlands, The Time of Your Life, Love's Old Sweet Song.
    New York: Harcourt, Brace, 1940.
Three Times Three. N.P.: The Conference Press, 1936.
Tracy's Tiger. Garden City, N.Y.: Doubleday, 1951.
The Trouble with Tigers. New York: Harcourt, Brace, 1950.
The Twin Adventures. New York: Harcourt, 1950.
The Whole Voyald and Other Stories. Boston: Little, Brown, 1956.

SECONDARY SOURCES

Angoff, Charles. *The Tone of the Twenties and Other Essays*. New York: Barnes and
    Noble, 1966.
Calonne, David. *William Saroyan*. Chapel Hill: University of North Carolina Press,
    1983.
Carpenter, Frederick I. "The Time of William Saroyan's Life." *Pacific Spectator*, 1
    (Winter 1947), 88-96.
Chapman, John. "Saroyan, Bless Him." *Theater Arts*, 42 (December 1958), 25-26.
Everding, Robert George. "The Dissolution Process in the Early Plays of William
    Saroyan." Unpublished dissertation, Stanford University, 1976.
Fisher, William J. "Whatever Happened to Saroyan." *College English*, 16 (March
    1955), 336-40.
Floan, Howard R. "Saroyan and Cervantes' Knight." *Thought*, 33 (Spring 1958), 81-92.
————. *William Saroyan*. New York: Twayne Publishers, 1966.
Justus, James H. "William Saroyan and the Theater of Transformation." *The Thirties*,
    ed. Warren French. Deland, Fla.: Everett Edwards, 1967.

Keyishian, Harry. "Michael Arlen and William Saroyan: Armenian Ethnicity and the Writer." *The Old Century and the New*, ed. Bruno Rosa. Rutherford, N.J.: Fairleigh-Dickinson, 1979.

Kherdian, David. *A Bibliography of William Saroyan: 1934-1966*. San Francisco: Roger Beacham, 1965.

Krickel, Edward. "Cozzens and Saroyan: A Look at Two Reputations." *Georgia Review*, 24 (Fall 1970), 281-96.

McGilligan, Patrick. "Mr. Saroyan's Thoroughly American Movie." *The Modern American Novel and the Movies*, ed. Gerald Peary and Roger Shatzkin. New York: Ungar, 1979.

Rhoads, Kenneth W. "Joe as Christ-Type in Saroyan's *The Time of Your Life*." *Essays in Literature*, 3 (Fall 1976), 227-43.

Sarkisian, Levon. "Saroyan's 'Rock Wagram': A Psycho-Social Character Study." *Armenian Review*, 11 (1959), 61-68.

Saroyan, Aram. *William Saroyan*. New York: Harcourt, Brace, Jovanovich, 1983.

Schulberg, Budd. "Saroyan: Ease and Unease on the Flying Trapeze." *Esquire*, 54 (October 1960), 85-91.

Shinn, Thelma J. "William Saroyan: Romantic Existentialist." *Modern Drama*, 15 (September 1972), 185-94.

Stern, Elaine Mary. "The Conservative Response amidst Decades of Change: Jack Kerouac and William Saroyan." Unpublished dissertation, Saint Louis University, 1976.

Straumann, Heinrich. *American Literature in the Twentieth Century*. London: Hutchinson's, 1951.

Tsusimoto, Ichiro. "William Saroyan, An Improvisator." *Kyushu American Literature*, 2 (May 1959), 12-16.

Wilson, Edmund. *The Boys in the Back Room*. Reprinted in *Classics and Commercials*. New York: Farrar, Straus, 1950.